NELSON'S LAST DIARY

Rear Admiral Lord Nelson at Vienna, 1800, *by Friedrich Heinrich Füger.*
(By courtesy of Mrs. John McCarthy)

NELSON'S LAST DIARY

A FACSIMILE EDITED BY

OLIVER WARNER

THE KENT STATE
UNIVERSITY PRESS

By Oliver Warner

A PORTRAIT OF LORD NELSON *1958*

NELSON'S BATTLES *1965*

THE LIFE & LETTERS OF VICE-ADMIRAL LORD COLLINGWOOD *1968*

International Standard Book Number 0 87338 121 1
Library of Congress Catalog Card Number 70-165752

First published 1971

Devised, designed and produced by Ruari McLean Associates, London
Printed in Great Britain by A. G. Bishop & Sons Ltd, Orpington, Kent
Bound in Great Britain by W. & J. Mackay & Co. Ltd, Chatham, Kent

simultaneously published in the United Kingdom by
Seeley, Service & Co. Ltd, London

Published by The Kent State University Press, Ohio

CONTENTS

ACKNOWLEDGEMENTS

Thanks are due to the authorities and staffs of the Public Record Office, the British Museum, the National Maritime Museum and the National Portrait Gallery for their courteous help in the preparation of this work: also to Mrs. John McCarthy for so kindly allowing the reproduction of the portrait which appears as frontispiece. The picture of H.M.S. *Victory* on the title-page is after a drawing by E. W. Cooke, engraved on steel by W. J. Cooke, from Southey's *Life of Nelson*, Bohn, 1861.

O.W.

To Ruari McLean

INTRODUCTION

> ' *Mercy, bright Spirit, I already feel*
> *The piercing edge of thy immortal steel* '
>
> DRYDEN: *Tyrannick Love*

The events of Nelson's last days, with which the Diary here reprinted is concerned, seem to have the inevitability of a Greek tragedy. Their outline is as familiar to those with an interest in history and biography as was the fable of Oedipus to an Athenian audience. What is remarkable is the tension at which Nelson recorded his thoughts, which rose to a climax of hope and acceptance in his famous prayer before Trafalgar. This was in the same strain in which the Diary had been begun. It echoed feelings to which he had given expression at other times during his career.

The urge to record is more typical of the artist than of any other type of man, and there is every sign that Nelson was an artist by temperament. To record was not a luxury but a necessity for him. Sometimes what he set down was for his own eyes alone; more often it was addressed to someone else; occasionally he seems to have had posterity in mind.

Among the Egerton Manuscripts at the British Museum there is a slip of paper on which is a note in Nelson's handwriting which reads as if he were totting up, for his private satisfaction, a sort of balance sheet of personal suffering. Like so much of what he wrote, it could have come from no other pen than his:

> ' *Wounds received by Lord Nelson:*
> His Eye in Corsica
> His Belly off Cape St. Vincent
> His Arm at Teneriffe.
> Tolerable for one war.'

The note is striking both for its facts and as an example of the satisfaction Nelson derived, all his life, from putting things down. He used to say that, next to doing great things, it was enviable to write a glorious account of them, and if proof were needed of how conscious an artist he was, it lies in the fact that he actually wrote out twice his final Prayer and, as is most probable, the whole of the rest of his Diary. He was determined that at least one copy should survive the battle. He had done the same sort of thing before, after the victory of the Nile, and his instinct was right. The world would surely be the poorer without such documents, for we should know Nelson less well than we do had they not been preserved.

II

It is sometimes asked how such men, whose schooling ashore generally ceased before their teens, contrived to write cogent prose. The answer is that they read and absorbed, ceaselessly, all their lives. Many of them, Nelson and Collingwood included, took Addison and Swift for models, and made no secret of the fact to their correspondents. Nelson loved Shakespeare and often quoted him, but above all else there was the King James Bible, that incomparable treasury, much of which they knew by heart, and whose cadences they heard repeatedly from lectern and pulpit.

Nelson, in an age noted for scepticism, had faith. The man he revered most in all his life was his clergyman father: he loved him; thought him the best of human beings. His devotion was expressed in letters home, especially those to his wife in the earlier years of their marriage. Fanny Nelson was greatly attached to her father-in-law, and she shared her husband's missives with him. Of what Edmund Nelson implanted in his son there is testimony from two very different occasions in the Admiral's life. They are not well known, and it is only of recent years that the manuscript of the first has been available to students.

It was composed in October 1793, shortly after Nelson, who then commanded the *Agamemnon*, had had an action with five French ships. Individually they were smaller than his own, but, together, much superior in aggregate of gun-power. He had been in contact for five hours, and would have continued but for serious damage to his masts and rigging. His ship, in the first of her many encounters during the long war with Revolutionary France, had one man killed and six wounded, and Nelson felt that the honours were with him. So did his officers, whom he had consulted before breaking off the engagement.

When the excitement was all over, and the enemy out of sight, Nelson opened his Sea Journal and wrote the following before he went to his cot:

'When I lay me down to sleep I recommend myself to the care of

> Almighty God. When awake I give myself up to His direction. Amidst all the evils that threaten me I will look up to Him for help and question not but that He will either avert them or turn them to my advantage. Though I know neither the time nor the manner of my death, I am not at all solicitous about it because I am sure that He knows them both, and that He will not fail to support and comfort me.'

Nearly eight years later, Nelson confided his thoughts in much the same way. During those years he had fought in the battle off Cape St Vincent which had brought his Commander-in-Chief, Jervis, an earldom, and Nelson a Knighthood of the Bath. He had also won his own superlative victory at Aboukir, an artist's battle if ever there was one. He had become a peer of the realm but had, alas, seen his marriage break up, after he had formed that ardent attachment to Emma Hamilton which was to be the cause of sadness among friends who had known Horatio and Fanny in their years together. His sternest battle, Copenhagen, was only recently behind him when he wrote to Emma Hamilton from the Baltic, on 8 May 1801, in a way which he was to repeat, more fully and movingly, on the eve of Trafalgar.

> 'I own myself a Believer in God, and if I have any merit in not fearing death, it is because I feel His power can shelter me when He pleases and that I must fall whenever it is His good pleasure.'

Such passages as these make nonsense of any idea that Nelson had suicide in mind on 21 October 1805. Premonition of death was quite another matter, and there are impressive indications that he felt it. To name but two: he told his sister Catherine Matcham, shortly before he embarked, about a gypsy prophecy in which he believed. Far more strikingly he said to Blackwood, captain of the frigate *Euryalus*, who was aboard the *Victory* receiving final instructions and who, together with Captain Hardy, witnessed the codicil to Nelson's will which formed part of the Diary, that he would never see him again. Two world wars, in which millions have been involved in front-line service, have afforded countless instances of similar prevision, so strong as to amount to certitude. Suicide, with its unfortunate connotations, would have had no part in the thoughts of such a man as Nelson. His private problems, considerable though they were, were certainly not such as to make him wish to end life: it was still sweet.

Every officer and man on the upper deck of the *Victory* ran the same risks that Nelson did, and it would have been unthinkable that he, their leader, should deliberately expose himself by reason of any personal troubles. No one has ever dared to suggest that Collingwood, Nelson's close friend, weary to exhaustion as he was with the gruelling work of blockade on which he had been engaged for many months without even the brief interlude at home that Nelson had enjoyed, longing for relief (death not excluded) had suicide in mind when he exposed himself, under the same conditions as Nelson, sailing at the head of his column in the *Royal Sovereign*. Collingwood came under murderous fire long before any other flag officer in the Fleet, and, as could have been expected, he had many narrow escapes. He was " thumped ", as he put it in letters home, more than once, and was actually hit in the leg by a splinter. He too had premonitions, though their particulars are unknown. A few weeks after the battle, he wrote to his wife in Northumberland:

> 'There is a thing which has made a considerable impression upon me. A week before the war, at Morpeth, I dreamed distinctly many of the circumstances of our late battle off the enemy's port, and I believe I told you of it at the time.'

When, towards the end of the action, he was informed by boat from the *Victory* of Nelson's mortal wound, grief rather than surprise was uppermost in his mind.

III

Concerning the main events in Nelson's life up to Trafalgar there is abundant, almost overwhelming material. The earlier years have never been more affectionately summed up than in a letter which Edmund Nelson wrote to the Reverend Brian Allott during the month of October 1798, soon after news of the Nile had become known to an astonished Europe.

> 'My great and good son went into the world without fortune,' wrote a proud parent, 'but with a breast replete with every moral and religious virtue: these have been his compass to steer by, and it has pleased God to be his shield in the day of battle, and to give success to his wishes to be of service to his Country. His Country seems sensible of his services, but should he ever meet with ingratitude, his scars will plead his cause: for at the

siege of Bastia he lost an eye: at Teneriffe an arm: on the memorable 14th of February he received a severe blow on his body, which he still feels; and now a wound on his head. After all this, you must allow his bloom of countenance must be faded, but the spirit beareth up yet as vigorous as ever. On the 29th of September he completed his 40th year, cheerful, generous and good; fearing no evil, because he has done none; an honour to grey my hairs, which with every mark of age creep upon me'.

It was at Calvi, not Bastia, that Nelson lost the sight of his right eye, though not the eye itself, and the 'memorable 14th of February', 1797, referred to the date of the battle of St Vincent. The 'wound in his head' resulting from a French shell at the Nile, though apparently superficial was for long troublesome, and it left a permanent mark on Nelson's forehead which he covered with a lock of hair.

Edmund Nelson's letter of 1798 was true when he wrote it, but he could not ever again have written of his son in quite such terms. Immediately after the Nile, Nelson sailed for Naples, and for nearly two years placed himself at the service of the Bourbon court. This led to little but trouble. His campaigning went wrong, and he grew so obsessed with Emma Hamilton, wife of his friend the British Minister, that he must soon have known that there could be no future with Fanny.

In July 1801 Nelson began his journey home, in company with the Hamiltons, by way of the Continent. He received adulation everywhere, and he sat to a number of artists, two of whom, Johann Schmidt of Dresden and Friedrich Heinrich Füger of Vienna, produced admirable though very differing portraits. Schmidt's was in pastel, and he made at least one almost perfect replica. He also painted Emma, in a version which became Nelson's particular favourite. There are those who consider that Schmidt's version of Nelson is as close to life as any rendering, except perhaps the wax effigy in Westminster Abbey. It conveys the private man. Füger's work was more grandiose, as was natural in one whose official post was Vice-Director of the Viennese Academy.

Füger's principal portrait (reproduced herein for the first time within the covers of a book), was long lost sight of, and has never been at all well known, though it is a work which, from an historical point of view, is of importance. It was bought in 1930 from a dealer who stated that it was from a private collection formerly in Hampstead. By a happy chance the present owner has an interest in and enthusiasm for everything concerning Nelson not exceeded by anyone in his own country or abroad.

The National Portrait Gallery has a portrait, also by Füger, which was acquired as long ago as 1859. It is the only fully documented representation of the admiral in plain clothes. This version is 19″ by 15½″: the uniformed picture is larger—27″ by 21¼″. It had always been something of a puzzle to know why the National Portrait Gallery version was not in uniform. The explanation seems to be that it was originally painted for the artist's own pleasure, not as a commission.

According to a document recorded in the archives of the Gallery, Nelson issued a banker's order, on 23 September 1800, to pay Füger the sum of £250 sterling when he delivered portraits of the Queen of Naples, Emma Hamilton and himself. He signed the order 'Brontë Nelson of the Nile', the style he used before he settled on 'Nelson and Brontë' to denote his English peerage and the Sicilian dukedom he had been given for services to King Ferdinand IV.

Füger must have been a hard worker if he produced the three paintings to which the document referred with speed, for Nelson was only a few weeks in Vienna on his way back from Italy. The Queen of Naples, Maria Carolina, had also journeyed there on a visit to her daughter, the Austrian Empress, and Nelson wished for some commemoration of the fact, hence his commission. The ladies were to be full length; his own picture was to be quarter-length. The artist was already known to the Neapolitan royal family, for he had worked at Caserta, the immense palace belonging to Ferdinand IV, where he executed a series of mural allegories on the Origin of the Sciences.

The more formal portrait resembles the London version, though neither have much affinity with other likenesses of the admiral. The insignia shown on the uniform (which is, correctly for the time, that of a rear admiral) are in all respects appropriate for the stage in Nelson's career when he sat. The stars of the three Orders of Chivalry are those of St Ferdinand, a Neapolitan decoration bestowed in 1799; the Order of the Crescent of Turkey, given in 1798 in recognition of the Battle of the Nile, and below it the Order of the Bath, which came to him in 1797 for services at St Vincent. Two large gold medals commemorate his leading part at St Vincent and the Nile.

Füger's son left a written statement (now in the National Portrait Gallery archives) that his father was so pleased with the result of his formal portrait that he did a head and shoulders for himself. This is almost certainly the one now in the Gallery. Although Füger's rendering is somewhat remote from the popular idea of Nelson, and far more solemn, it is not more so than a whole series which had been produced a little earlier in Sicily. Füger worked from life, and his portraits deserve respect as first-hand evidence. He conveyed an impression of leadership and decision which were strong characteristics in a complex personality.

IV

Nelson's later services, in the Baltic in 1801, then commanding the anti-invasion forces which were kept in readiness for as long as Napoleon maintained an army on the far side of the Channel, and finally, after the brief Peace of Amiens, as Commander-in-Chief, Mediterranean, confirmed him as a national figure as well as a general favourite. He had bought Merton, a property in Surrey which he shared with the Hamiltons, where he lived in great contentment during the months he was at home. Sir William Hamilton died just as Nelson was recalled to active service, and for over two years the *Victory*, in the Mediterranean and Atlantic, was his stately home.

During the early months of 1805, having pursued a combined Franco-Spanish fleet from the Mediterranean to the West Indies and back to Europe, Nelson returned to England, anchoring on 18 August. He was ashore until 14 September, and sailed from Spithead next day. It is with the events of 13 September to 21 October that the Diary is concerned; rejoining the Fleet with some reinforcements; contact with other ships; the detachment of Rear Admiral Louis, and vessels in need of provisions, to Gibraltar, and a bare outline of operational movements. Apart from the opening and the close, the Diary is really more what Dr Beatty, surgeon of the *Victory*, called it, a memorandum book, such as Nelson usually kept when at sea.

The fuller details of the Trafalgar campaign, including its climax with the emergence of the Franco-Spanish Fleet under Villeneuve, the battle which resulted, and its aftermath, are set down, largely in documentary form, in the seventh and last volume of Sir Harris Nicolas's great collection of Nelson's *Dispatches and Letters*, as well as in scores of biographies.

The history of the Diary or memorandum book with which this account is concerned is strange, and it has recently been traced in some detail by Winifred Gérin in her substantial biography of Horatia, Nelson's daughter by Emma Hamilton, who, together with her mother, was left a legacy to the nation. It was certainly one of the oddest ' legacies ' on record, and that it was never honoured has been a source of worry ever since. There were reasons why this was the case, and there is one most important fact to be remembered. At the time of the events concerned, the country was in the middle of one of the most protracted wars in history, fighting for its future, and much that has long been common knowledge was still secret.

The gist of the codicil was a case very much in point. Nelson rested Emma's claim upon the gratitude of the nation on two incidents, neither of them at all satisfactory. The first was that she had received early information, through her friendship with the Queen of Naples, of Spanish intention to declare war on Britain as the ally of France. This fact was of no consequence, as the Foreign Office in London already possessed equally good information, drawn from less devious sources. The second was quite absurd. Nelson argued that it had been Emma's influence at the Neapolitan Court which had eased the granting of supplies to Nelson's squadron when the Admiral put in at Sicily during the Nile campaign. In fact, in the face of such strength as Nelson commanded, the local authorities had no alternative but to meet his needs. Had they made any serious attempt to frustrate him, Nelson and his sailors would have helped themselves, making scrupulous payment for what they took. As a sea commander, Nelson was a realist, and knew this well enough. As a lover he was obsessed, and he came to believe a great deal of nonsense which Emma imparted over the years, and especially during their time together in Italy.

On the financial plane, Emma was well off, and so, in a more modest way, was little Horatia. Nelson had already left his child £4,000, which was to be administered by Emma. As for Emma, she had been left an annuity of £800 by her husband, of which £100 was to be paid to her mother, Mrs Cadogan, while she lived. Nelson himself left Emma the handsome property at Merton, together with £2,000 and an annuity of £500 charged on his Brontë estate. Any reasonable woman would have considered herself lucky in a purely worldly sense, but the plain fact was that Emma's affairs were already in confusion, and growing steadily worse. The only restraining hand was that of Mrs Cadogan, who kept her daughter's budget as straight as she could, which was never saying much.

If the Government had honoured Nelson's wishes, besides providing handsomely for his family, as indeed it did, this could only have been done through the Secret Service fund, or as a special favour granting Emma a continuation of the pension that Sir William Hamilton had enjoyed as a former Minister, but which had ceased on his death. Had either course been taken, it would have created a very difficult precedent indeed, one which no Government could readily have contemplated. It is true that in those days some very odd things were done, financially, in the way of personal emolument and relief, but always with the active concurrence of the King or a political party. Emma Hamilton had no political standing whatever, and George III had little use for Nelson's private way of life. He preferred him at sea, as did the Board of Admiralty: there, he never made extravagant claims, and always seemed to perform prodigies and sometimes miracles.

Even supposing that Pitt, who warmly admired Nelson, but who died soon after Trafalgar, had been able to do something for Emma, the ultimate result, it is certain, would have been the same. Emma would have disintegrated just as fast and inevitably as she did. For she was no more capable of looking after money, however much or little she had, than the stout party who was later to become the Prince Regent. The difference was that Prinny, by accident of birth, could draw upon the resources of the country to help him out when, at various crises in his life, he had got deep into debt. Emma could not. Otherwise they were much alike. Old Lord Bristol, peer and bishop, had exclaimed on meeting Emma: "God Almighty must have been in a glorious mood when he made you!" He would scarcely have made the same remark in 1805, by which time anyone with real knowledge of Emma would have known that, with Nelson gone, there was no hope for anything but a long slide down-hill, with no alleviation, as Prinny was always able to manage, in the way of Parliamentary grants.

Yet Emma had many faithful friends, as post-Trafalgar events were to show: in fact, for the remaining ten years of her life she was not only her own worst enemy, but often her only one. The codicil was not disregarded through lack of assiduity on the part of well-wishers; where they were ham-strung was because implementation was no one's *particular* business, and because Emma was so incorrigibly careless and indiscreet. For instance, Nelson enjoined her to burn his letters. Emma not only did nothing of the sort, but her negligence resulted in the final ruin of her own reputation, and brought much discredit upon Nelson. The compensation is that posterity has been enabled to follow the entire course of Nelson's liaison and its consequences, which in its own way is as remarkable as his life at sea. If it deprives him for ever of the character of plaster saint, and altered the character perceived by his father in 1798, it affords an enthrallingly full idea of what may happen to a susceptible man, given the extraordinary circumstances of Nelson's later life.

V

After Nelson's death, Hardy, as captain of the *Victory*, took charge of all his possessions on board, including the Diary. The news of the battle became known in London on 6 November and on 13 November Lady Elizabeth Foster visited Emma at her London house in Clarges Street. Emma was in bed, with " the appearance of a person stunned," and with Nelson's latest letters strewn all around. Lord Barham, the First Lord of the Admiralty, had sent Fanny Nelson a letter in his own hand, announcing her husband's death. Emma, and the principal members of the admiral's family, were informed by letter from the Comptroller of the Navy. Emma received her note at Merton by way of Captain Whitby, an Admiralty messenger.

Nelson's solicitor, Haslewood, took Nelson's will and the known codicils to Doctor's Commons to be registered and it was not until 4 December, when the *Victory* arrived off St Helens, Isle of Wight, that the existence of a final codicil was even suspected. Hardy had never been a partisan of Emma's, but any doubt of his kindness towards her was removed by the assiduity and feeling with which he forwarded Nelson's personal possessions, which he sent by Captain Blackwood. Emma was still in bed when they arrived, and within a few days Lionel Goldsmid, who had one great ambition, to serve in Nelson's ship—he was then eight years old—was regaled with an astonishing sight. " The very coat," he later reported, " in which the dear old Admiral was dressed in the fatal battle and received his death wound was on the outside of the bed—the hole where the bullet passed through stiffened with congealed blood." Emma was extracting every scrap of drama from " the dear old Admiral " (Nelson was a youthful 47 when he died)—and it was a great deal. No one ever accused her of delicacy.

Hardy's duty had been to remit the codicil to Nelson's legal representative. This was his brother William, who was a Prebendary of Canterbury and now, by the King's favour, Earl Nelson. He also journeyed to Lymington to consult George Rose, who offered to submit the matter to Pitt as Prime Minister. The Earl had no objection to extracts being made, among the recipients being Prinny, who expressed great sympathy with Nelson's wishes.

Pitt's unexpected death, on 23 January 1806, caused the matter to be remitted to his successor, Lord Grenville, from whom Nelson had warned Emma she could look for nothing. The new Prime Minister kept the Diary and codicil for four months and then returned it to Haslewood. By that time handsome grants had been made to Nelson's family, and it had become clear that Emma could expect nothing from Parliamentary sources. Earl Nelson thereupon gave Emma the Diary and codicil, which she promptly registered at Doctor's Commons. The gesture was useless. The document could only be honoured at Government level, and it would for ever be disregarded.

There was one last little ceremony before the matter was officially closed, and the Diary stored away among the archives. On 11 July 1806 the Rev. Dr Alexander Scott, Nelson's devoted chaplain, swore an affidavit in the Prerogative Court of Canterbury whose text is printed herein as an appendix to the Diary.

VI

That Nelson made two copies of his Diary is shown by the fact that Sir Harris Nicolas in 1846 worked from what he described as 'An Autograph or fac simile copy in the possession of P. Toker Esq.' Much of this copy seems to have disappeared though there is a portion, including entries for 13 September 1805 and the following day, and for 20 October and the following day (including the Prayer and codicil) in the National Maritime Museum, Greenwich. It is probably part of the legacy of Nelson memorials which Emma dissipated or pledged in her later and distressful years. It is clearly a second copy, in Nelson's own hand, and not any kind of mechanical copy, tracing, or copy by a secretary. It is now bound and arranged so as to pull out and be viewed at a stretch.

The first or official autograph is preserved in a special box at the

Public Record Office, to which it was transferred in 1962 from Somerset House, where for years it was deposited alongside Shakespeare's will. In 1917, at a time of national crisis in war, it was thoughtfully printed by Gilbert Hudson, otherwise known as an elocutionist, with an Introduction and notes. Hudson observed that at some stage entries had been extracted, probably as souvenirs, for there is a gap from 3 to 7/8 October and another comprising most of the entry for 20 October. The first, and happily less important, lacuna is probably there for ever, but the whole of the entry for 20 October can fortunately be made good from Nicolas, who this time worked from an 'Autograph in the possession of J. Wild Esq.' thus indicating that Emma's copy had been divided between Toker and Wild, to mention two earlier collectors whose names are known for certain.

Gilbert Hudson's edition of the Diary has long been out of print and is now scarce. He made only a few errors in transcription, though one is of some note. In the entry for 9 October 1805 he printed: "Sent Adl. Collingwood the Nelson Touch." It was as if Nelson was performing magic on his second-in-command. Hudson erred in good company in getting the word wrong, for Beatty, surgeon of the *Victory*, in his *Authentic Narrative of the Death of Lord Nelson* (1807) printed the words as 'the Nelson truth', which was equally wide of the mark. Nicolas preferred Touch, referring to the well-known 'Nelson Touch'—the explanation of his proposed battle tactics with which the Commander-in-Chief electrified his captains.

As was so often the case, it was left to Collingwood to clear the matter up in a satisfactory way. He wrote in his copy of Dr Beatty's account, which is now at Greenwich: "it was the Nelson *trunk*—which passed with Papers and letters between us each having a key." With that elucidation in mind it is hard to see how Nelson's handwriting, usually so clear, could have been so mistaken. But that is hindsight.

There are a handful of characters whose interest seems to grow rather than diminish with the passage of time. Among men of war, Napoleon, Nelson and Wellington are among those of whom it seems impossible to learn too much. In one respect, Nelson was singularly fortunate. Like Wolfe, the general he so much admired, he died at the height of his glory, and as George III said to Earl Nelson when he returned his brother's Insignia of the Order of the Bath: "He died the death he wished."

Emma fared badly. Her mother pre-deceased her, and she died of drink at Calais in 1815, debt-ridden, and attended by Horatia, who could never bring herself to believe that the woman who had tried her so much was really her mother. Horatia survived into old age, looking the image of her father, and in mid-century the nation, headed by the Prince Consort, at last did something to honour Nelson's request by way of help to her family. For Horatia Nelson Ward, as she then was, had become the wife of a clergyman of slender means, a man cast in much the same mould as Nelson's father. She had had her trials, but she was a happy woman, as Nelson would have wished.

NELSON'S LAST DIARY

Transcribed from the copy in the Public Record Office, London

Not to be registered to the
Words October the twenty
first one thousand eight
hundred and five*

Geo : Silk
Proctor

[*p. 28 in this transcription.]

Friday night at half
past Ten drove from
dear dear Merton
where I left all which
I hold dear in this World
to go and serve my King
& Country May the
Great God whom I adore
enable me to fullfill
the expectations of my
Country and if it is His
good pleasure that I
should return my thanks
will never cease being

offerred up to the throne of
His Mercy, If it is His
good providence to cut
short my days upon
Earth I bow with the
greatest submission
relying that He will
protect those so dear
to me that I may leave
behind. His will will be
done amen amen
amen.

Saturday Sept. 14th: 1805—
at Six o'clock arrived at
Portsmouth and having
arrainged all my business
embarked at the Bathing
Machines with Mr. Rose
and Mr. Canning at
2 got on board the Victory
at St. Helens who dined
with me preparing
for sea

Sunday Sept. 15th: 1805
at day weighed with
light airs Northerly
at 6 was obliged to
anchor at 8 weighed
all day Light breezes
at sun sett off Christ
Church all night Light
Breezes & very foggy Euryalus
in Company

---

wrote Ly. Hn.
Monday Sept. 16th. first
part Light Breezes &
very foggy at noon

fresh Breezes Westerly in
the evening off the Berry
head 4 miles. all night
fresh Breezes Westerly

---

wrote Ly. Hn.
Tuesday Sept. 17th: fresh
Breezes WSW at 9 abreast
of Plyo. sent in Euryalus

to call out the ajax and
Thunderer all night standg
to the Westward Wind from
SW to SSW

---

wrote Ly H.
Wednesday Sept. 18 first
part Light Breezes & heavy
Western Swell Wind South
Lay too for the ajax and

Thunderer Lizard North
at Noon they joined made
all possible Sail all night
Breezes Vble from SE to SSW
Swell from the Westward

Thursday Sept. 19th first part
fresh gales & heavy sea
at noon hard gales at SW
at 6 PM hard Rain wind
at NW all night heavy
Sea & fresh breezes

---

wrote Ly. Hn.
Friday Sept. 20th. Modte
Breezes WSW & heavy Sea
at 9 Saw a Squadron of

Ships of War at 11 passed the
Squadron of Rear Adl. Stirling
consisting of 5 sail of the line
and one frigate at noon
Wind WSW saw a frigate
to Windward which made
the private signal at 2
Spoke the Decade carrying
the Flag of Rear Adl. Sir
Richd. Bickerton Capt. Stuart
came on board gave him
orders for his farther proceedgs.
fresh gales at 3 reeft the
Courses all night very fresh
gales from the NW which
came on with heavy rain
at 7 o'clock.

Saturday Sept. 21st. 1805.
fresh gales all day at NNW
at night wind at North &
NE heavy swell

Sunday Sept. 22nd. Modte
Breezes at NE & heavy swell
from NW at 1 o'clock
saw a Convoy of 7 Sail
under a Vessel of War in
the SE quarter at 6 o'clock
Euryalus made the Signal
that a Vessel was reconnoi
tering in the East quarter
all night fresh gales at
East to ESE.

Monday Sept. 23rd. fresh gales
E b S at 6 o'clock abreast of
Cape Finisterre 17 Lgs at noon
modte W. in Latde. 42°. 2′5 N
all night fine Weather
wind Easterly

Tuesday Sept. 24th. Modte.
Breezes SE at noon in
Latd. 40:05 N: 3 pm
Light airs South in the
evening wind Northerly
Light Breezes all night
at NE and a Swell from
the NW

wrote Ly. H.
Wednesday Sept. 25th. 1805
Light airs Southerly
saw the Rock of Lisbon
SSE 10 Leagues at sun sett
the Capt. of the Constance
came on board sent my
letters for England by him
to Lisbon and wrote to
Capt. Sutton & the Consul
the Enemys fleet had
not left Cadiz the 18th: of
this month therefore I
yet hope they will wait
my arrival

Monday Sept. 26th: Light
airs at NW all day
Rock of Lisbon in sight
to the NNE 13—14 Lgs:
at 4 o'clock sent Euryalus
to join Vice Adl. Collingwood
with my orders to put himself
under Command con-
sidering myself as within
the Limits of my Command
at night Light Breezes
at NW

Friday Sept. 27th 1805 at
day Light Cape St. Vincent
SE b S by compass 6 Leagues
saw a Sloop of War or
small frigate East 5 or 6
miles called her in She
proved to be the Nautilus
Sloop from Vice Adl.
Collingwood bound to
England with dispatches
at noon abreast of Lagos
Bay fresh Breezes NW
at 1 am brought too
fresh Breezes NW b N.

Saturday Sept. 28th: 1805
fresh Breezes at NNW
at daylight bore up &
made sail at 9 saw the
Aetna cruizing at noon
saw nine Sail of ships of
War bearing East Latd:
36° 32N at one saw
eighteen Sail nearly Calm
in the Evening joined the fleet
under Vice admiral Collinwd:
saw the Enemys fleet in
Cadiz amounting to 35 or 36
Sail of the Line

Sunday Sept: 29th: fine Weathr.
gave out the necessary orders
for the fleet sent Euryalus
to watch the Enemy with
the Hydra off Cadiz.

Monday Sept: 30th fine
Weather Wind Easterly

Tuesday Oct: 1st: fine Wr.
Ald: Louis's Squadron joined
with Thunder & Endymion
with sprung masts, sent
Aetna to cruize under Cape
St Marys Pickle joined
from Plymouth.

Wrote Ly H:
Wednesday Octr 2nd:
fine Wr: Westerly sent
Thunder to Gibr: Sarda:

Palermo & Naples, sent
Canopus, Tigre, Spencer
Queen, Zealous to Gibr. &
Tetuan for water & provn:
Sent the Nimble to
England all night fine
weather

Thursday Oct: 3rd: 1805
fine Weather sent
Eurydice to Cruize under
Cape St: Marys

off Cadiz, Eurydice captured
a Spanish Privateer.

Wednesday Oct 9th: fresh
Breezes Easterly received an
account from Capt. Black-
wood that the french ships
had all bent their topgt. sails
sent the Pickle to him with
orders to keep a good look out.
sent adl: Collingwood the
Nelson Trunk—at night
Wind Westerly

Monday oct: 10th; 1805
fine Wr: Wind Westerly
receiv'd an account that
the Enemy are ready for

Sea and at the very
harbours mouth. Bellisle
made her number at noon
Bellisle joind from Plyh:
in the Evening the Renommee
frigate & Confounder G Brig
sent the Aetna & Confounder
to Gibralter. all night very

fresh Breezes NW & Rain

Friday Oct: 11th: fresh
Breezes NW

Saturday Oct: 12th: fresh
Breezes NWerly keeping
to the Westward. ~~Renommee
joined~~

wrote Ly: Hn.
Sunday Oct. 13th: 1805
fine weather Agamem-
:non joined from
England having fallen
in with the french
Squadron off Cape Finistr.
consisting of 1 three decker
and 5 two decked ships
and had a narrow
escape from Capture

L'Aimable also joined
who had likewise been
chased Prince of Wales
sailed for England

Monday Octr: 14th:
fine Weather Westerly
Wind sent Amphion
to Gibralter & algiers
enemy at the Harbours
mouth placed Defence &
agamemnon from Seven
to Ten Leagues West of Cadiz
and Mars & Colossus five
Leagues East from the
fleet whose station will be
from 15 Lgs: to twenty West
of Cadiz and by this Chain

I hope to have a constant
communication with the

frigates off Cadiz

Tuesday Octr. 15th: fine Wr
Westerly sent Renommee
& L'aimable to Gibralter
& Malta. and the transp^ts.
to Gibr. Adl Louis is ordered
to see the Convoy above
Carthegena & the frigates
to escort them to Malta.
all night modte. Breezes.
Westerly

Wednesday Octr. 16th.
Modte: Breezes Westerly
all the forenoon employd
forming the fleet into the

order of Sailing at noon
fresh Breezes WSW & squally
in the evening fresh gales
Enemy as before, by sign:
from Weazle

Thursday Octr. 17th: 1805
Mode: Breze. N Werly
sent Donegal to Gibralter
to get a ground Tier of Casks
receivd accounts by the
Diligent storeship that
Sir Richd. Strachan was
supposed in sight of the
french Rochford Squadron
which I hope is true

at midnight the wind came
to the Eastward

---

friday Octr. 18th. fine weather
wind Easterly the combined
fleets cannot have finer Wr:
to put to sea.

Saturday Octr. 19th. fine Wr.
wind Easterly at ½ pt: 9
the Mars being one of the
look out ships made the
signal that the Enemy were
coming out of Port made the
signal for a general Chase
SE. Wind at South Cadiz
bearing ESE by Compass
distance 16 Leagues.

at three the Colossus made
the signal that the Enemys
fleet was at Sea in the
evening made sigls: to observe
my motions during the
night, for the Britannia
Prince & Dreadnought they
being heavy sailors to take
stations as convenient
and for Mars, Orion Bellisle
Leviathan, Bellerophon &
Polyphemus to go ahead
during the night and to
carry a light standing
for the streights mouth

at 5 telegraphed Capt: Bd.
that I rely'd upon his
keeping sight of the Enemy
at 5 o'clock Naiad made
the signal for 31 sail of
the Enemy NNE. the
frigates and Look out

ships kept sight of the
Enemy most admirably
all night and told me
by Signals which tack
they were upon. at
8 We wore & Stood to the
SW and at 5 am Wore

and stood to the NE

Monday Octr: 21st 1805
at day Light saw the
Enemys Combined fleet
from East to ESE bore
away made the signal
for order of sailing and
to prepare for Battle the
Enemy with their heads
to the Southward, at 7
the Enemy wearing in
succession, May the Great
God whom I worship
Grant

to my Country and for
the benefit of Europe
in General a great and
Glorious Victory, and may
no misconduct in any
one tarnish it, and
May humanity after
Victory be the predomi
-nant feature in the
British fleet. For
myself individually
I commit my Life
to Him who made

me, and may his blessing
light upon my endea-

-vours for serving my
Country faithfully, to
Him I resign myself
and the Just cause which
is entrusted to me to
Defend—
Amen, Amen, Amen

[*The Codicil*]

October the twenty first
one thousand Eight hundred
and five then is sight of
the Combined fleets of
France and Spain distant
about Ten miles.

Whereas the Eminent
Services of Emma
Hamilton Widow of the
Right Honourable Sir
William Hamilton
have been of the very
greatest Service to Our
King & Country to my

knowledge without her
receiving any reward
from either our King
or Country, first that she
obtained the King of Spains
letter in 1796 to His
Brother the King of
Naples acquainting him
of his intention to Declare
War against England
from which letter the
ministry sent out orders
to then Sir John Jervis
to Strike a Stroke if oppor:

tunity offered against
either the arsenals of

Spain or her fleets—that
neither of these was done
is not the fault of Lady
Hamilton the opportu-
-nity might have been
offered, secondly the British
fleet under my Com-
-mand could never have
returned the second time
to Egypt had not Lady
Hamiltons influence
with the Queen of Naples

caused Letters to be wrote
to the Governor of Syracuse
that he was to encourage
the fleet being supplied
with everything should
they put into any Port
in Sicily. We put into
Syracuse and received
every supply went to
Egypt & destroyed the
French fleet. Could I have
rewarded these Services I
would not now call upon
my Country but as that

has not been in my
power I leave Emma
Lady Hamilton therefore
a Legacy to my King and
Country that they will
give her an ample
provision to maintain
her Rank in Life. I
also leave to the benefi-
-cence of my Country
my adopted daughter
Horatia Nelson Thomp-

-son and I desire She
Will

Use in future the name
of Nelson only, these
are the only favors I
ask of my King and
Country at this moment
when I am going to
fight their Battle
May God. Bless My
King & Country and
all those who I hold
dear My Relations
it is needless to mention

they will of course be
amply provided for
Nelson & Bronte

Witness
Henry Blackwood
T M Hardy

Proved at London the 11th day of July
1806 before the Right Honorable Sir William
Scott Knt Dr of Laws & Surrate by the Oaths
of the Reverend & Right Honorable William
Nelson Dr in Divinity Viscount Merton & Earl
Nelson of Trafalgar & William Haslewood
Esqr the Exors named in the will to whom
admin was granted having been first
sworn duly to admr. The will with seven
codicils was Proved the 23rd of December
last by the said Executors.

Will & Codls }
reg^d. Dec 1805 }

THE AFFIDAVIT

Extracted from the Principal Registry of the Probate Divorce and Admiralty Division of the High Court of Justice.

In the Prerogative Court of Canterbury.

The following is a copy Affidavit annexed to the Will of the Right Honourable Horatio Lord Viscount Nelson deceased proved 11th July, 1806, but forming no part of the Probate.

30TH JUNE, 1806.

APPEARED PERSONALLY the Reverend ALEXANDER JOHN SCOTT of St. John's College in the University of Cambridge & Vicar of South Minster in the county of Essex Doctor in Divinity and made Oath that he the Deponent on the 21st day of October in the year 1805 & for sometime preceding was Chaplain on board his Majestys Ship *Victory* one of the Squadron under the Command of the late Right Honorable Horatio Lord Viscount Nelson deceased and this Deponent says that during an Action on the day aforesaid between His said Majesty's Squadron & the Combined Fleets of France & Spain off Trafalgar the said Lord Viscount Nelson having been mortally wounded in the said Action soon after the same happened addressed himself to this Deponent and sayd "I am dying Doctor remember me to Lady Hamilton remember me to Horatio tell Lady * [Ham]ilton I have made a will and left her & Horatio a legacy * [to my] Country" And this Deponent says that the said Deceased * [sever]al times in the course of the same Day made declaration in the hearing of and to this Deponent to the same effect and having on the same day departed this life he the Deponent was present on board the said Ship with Sir Thomas Masterman Hardy Baronet then Thomas Masterman Hardy Esquire Captain of the said Ship

* Here a fragment of the paper is missing.

when they found in the escrutoire of the said Deceased a Book wherein amongst other things are the words following to wit October the Twenty first one thousand eight hundred and five then in sight of the Combined Fleets of France and Spain distant about ten miles also the words "I leave Emma Lady Hamilton therefore a legacy to my King and Country that they will give her an ample provision to maintain her Rank in life I also leave to the beneficence of my country my adopted daughter Horatia Nelson Thompson" and ending "my relations it is needless to mention they will of course be amply provided for" and thus subscribed "Nelson & Bronte" and this Deponent says that having carefully viewed the Book hereto annexed marked A wherein the several words before recited appear the same is the identical Book found in the escrutoire aforesaid in the hand writing of the said deceased and that * believes meant & referred to by the deceased and his aforesaid declarations.

Same day the said ALEXANDER JOHN
SCOTT Doctor in Divinity aforesaid
was duly sworn to the truth hereof. A. J. SCOTT.

Before me.

GEORGE OGILVIE

Surrogate

Pre[t] GEO. SILK

Not. Pub.

* Here a few words have been worn out.

NELSON'S LAST LETTER TO LADY HAMILTON

Victory Octr. 19th: 1805 Noon Cadiz ESE 16 Leagues

My Dearest beloved Emma the dear friend of my bosom the Signal has been made that the Enemys Combined fleet are coming out of Port. We have very little Wind so that I have no hopes of seeing them before to-morrow May the God of Battles crown my endeavours with success at all events I will take care that my name shall ever be most dear to you and Horatia both of whom I love as much as my own life. and as my last writing before the battle will be to you so I hope in God that I shall live to finish my letter after the Battle. May Heaven bless you prays your Nelson & Bronte. Octr. 20th, in the morning we were close to the mouth of the Streights but the Wind had not come far enough to the Westward to allow the Combined Fleets to Weather the shoals off Traflagar but they were counted as far as forty Sail of Ships of War which I suppose to be 34 of the Line and six frigates, a Group of them was seen off the Lighthouse of Cadiz this Morng but it blows so very fresh & thick weather that I rather believe they will go into the Harbour before night. May God Almighty give us success over these fellows and enable us to get a Peace

[*The letter was unfinished and on the last leaf Emma Hamilton added the words:*]

This letter was found open on His desk and brought to Lady Hamilton by Capn. Hardy. Oh miserable wretched Emma
Oh glorious & happy Nelson

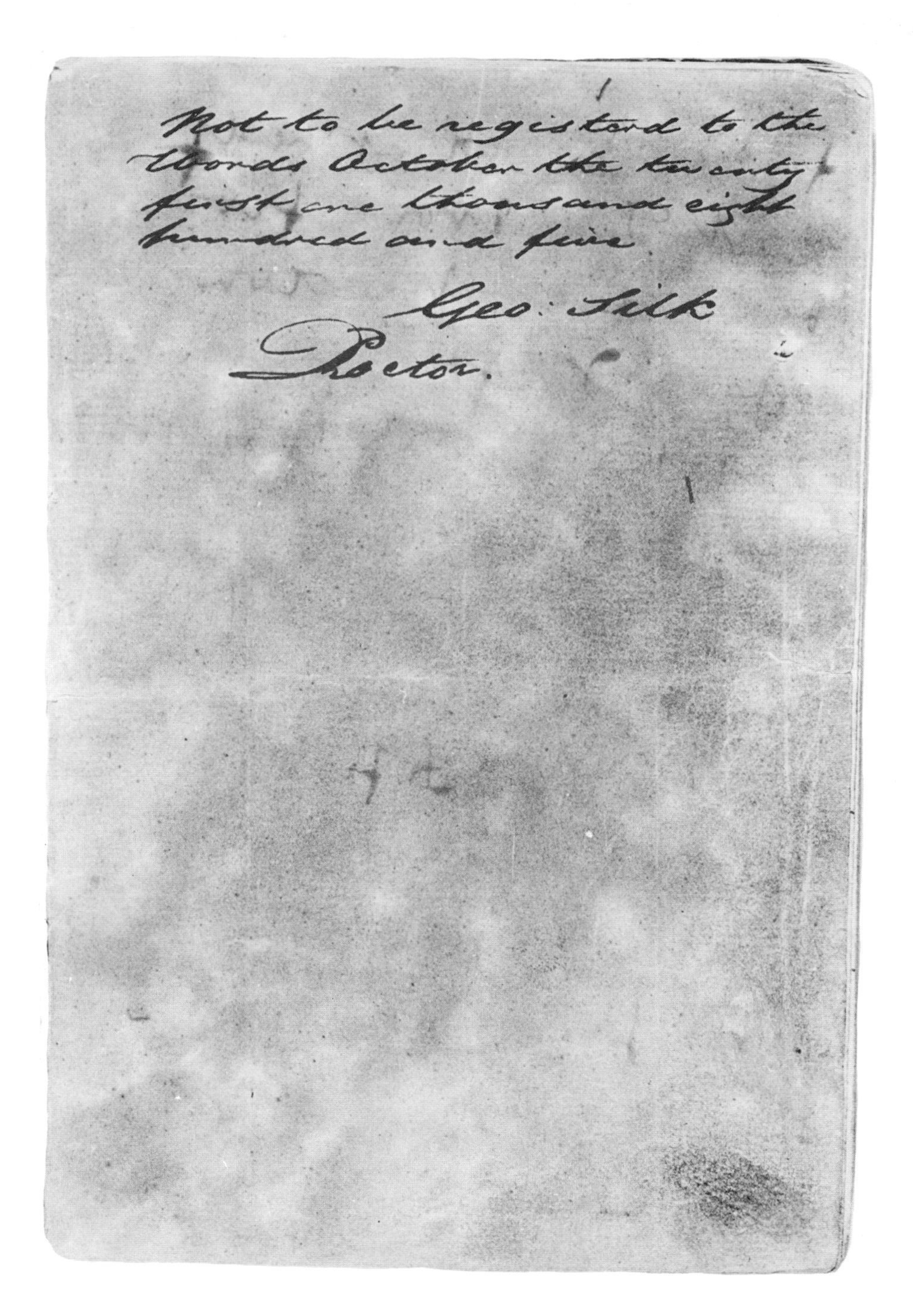
Not to be registerd to the words October the twenty first one thousand eight hundred and five

Geo: Silk
Rector.

2

Friday night at half
past Ten I drove from
dear dear Melton
where I left all which
I hold dear in this world
to serve my King
Country. May the
Great God whom I adore
enable me to fulfill
the expectations of my
Country and if it is His
good pleasure that I
should return my thanks
will never cease being

offered up to the throne of
His mercy. If it is His
good providence to cut
short my days upon
Earth I bow with the
greatest submission
relying that He will
protect those so dear
to me that I may leave
behind. His will be
done amen amen
amen

Saturday Sept. 14th: 1805 —
at Six O'Clock arrived at
Portsmouth and having
arranged all my business
embarked at the Bathing
Machines with Mr. Rose
and Mr. Canning at
2 got on board the Victory
at St. Helens who dined
with me preparing
for Sea

Sunday Sept: 15th: 1805
at day weighed with
Light air Northerly
at 6 was obliged to
anchor at 8 weighed
all day Light Breezes
at sun set off Christ
church all night Light
Breezes & very foggy Euryal[us]
in Company

---

wrote Li[illegible]
Monday Sept: 16th: first
part Light Breezes &
very foggy at noon

fresh Breezes Westerly in
the evening off the Berry
head 4 miles all night
fresh Breezes westerly

Tuesday Sept: 17: fresh
Breezes WSW at 9 abreast
of Ply: sent in Euryalus
beat out the ajax and
Thunderer all night stand
to the westward wind from
SW to SSW

Wednesday Sept: 18 first
part light Breezes & heavy
weather Squalls wind South
Lay too for the ajax and

Wensdays Lizard North
at Noon they Joined make
all possibel Sail at Night
Breezes Vble from SE & SSW
Swell from the Westward

Thursday Sept: 19th: first part
fresh Gales & heavy Sea
at Noon hard Gales at SW
at 6 PM hard Rain wind
at NW all Night heavy
Sea & fresh Breezes

---

mod Sept: 21th
Friday Sept: 20: Mod:
Breezes WSW & heavy Sea
at 9 Saw a Squadron of

Ships of War at 11 passed the
Squadron of Rear Adl. Sterling
consisting of 5 Sail of the Line
and one frigate at noon
Wind W.N.W Saw a frigate
to Windward which made
the private signal at 2
Spoke the Decade carrying
the Flag of Rear Adl. Sir
Richd. Bickerton Capt. Stuart
came on board gave him
orders for his farther proceedg.
fresh gales at 3 reefed the
Courses all night very fresh
Gales from the NW which
came on with heavy rain
at 9 O'Clock

Saturday Sept. 21st 1805 –
fresh gales all day at Night
at night wind at North &
NE heavy swell

Sunday Sept. 22nd: mod.
Breezes at NE & heavy Swell
from NW at 1 O'Clock
saw a Convoy of 7 Sail
under a Vessel of war in
the SE quarter at 6 O'Clock
Euryalus made the Signal
that a Vessel was reconnoi-
tring in the East quarter
all night fresh gales at
East bNE –

Monday Sept: 23rd: fresh gales
E b S at 6 oClock abreast of
Cape Finisterre 17 Lgs. at noon
Dist: W: in Latd: 42: 25 N
all the first fine weather
wind Easterly

Tuesday Sept: 24th: mod:
Breezes SE at noon in
Latd: 40: 05 No: 3 Pm
light airs South in the
evening wind Northerly
Light Breezes all night
at NE and a swell from
the NW

wrote Ld. B.
Wednesday Septr. 25th 1805
Light airs Southerly
saw the Rock of Lisbon
SSE 10 Leagues at Sun Sett
the Captn. of the Constance
came onboard sent my
letters for England by him
to Lisbon and wrote to
Captn. Sutton & the Consul
the Enemys fleet had
not left Cadiz the 18th of
this month therefore I
yet hope they will wait
my arrival

12

Monday Feb. 26th Light
airs at NW all day
Rock of Lisbon in sight
bore NNE 13 Lgs
at 4 o'clock sent Euryalus
to join Vice Adl. Collingwood
with my orders & put himself
under my Command con:
:sidering myself as within
the limits of my Command
at noon Light Breezes
at NW

Friday Septr. 27th 1805 at
Day Light Cape St. Vincent
SEbS by Compass 6 Leagues
Saw a Sloop of War or
Small frigate East 5 or 6
miles called her in She
proved to be the Nautilus
Sloop from Vice Adm.
Collingwood bound to
England with dispatches
at noon abreast of Lagos
Bay fresh Breezes NW
at 1 am brought too
fresh Breezes NWbN

14

Saturday Septr. 28th: 1805
fresh breezes at NbW
at daylight bore up and
made sail at 9 saw the
Aetna cruizing at noon
saw nine sail of ships of
war bearing East Latd:
36:32 N at one saw
eighteen sail nearly calm
in the evening joined the fleet
under Vice admiral Collingwood
saw the enemys fleet in
Cadiz amounting to 35 or 36
sail of the Line

Sunday Sept: 29th: fine weather
gave out the necessary orders
for the fleet sent Euryalus
to watch the Enemy with
the Hydra off Cadiz -

Monday Sept: 30th: fine
weather wind Easterly

Tuesday Oct: 1st: fine Wr.
Ad: Louis's Squadron Joined
with Number of [illegible]
with Fresh Meats, sent
Aetna [illegible] under Cape
St Marys Pickle Joined
from Plymouth

mod. W. N.
Wednesday Octr. 2nd.
fine Wr. Westerly sent
Munder to Gibr. Sardª.
Palermo & Naples, sent
Canopus, Tigre, Spencer
Queen, Zealous to Gibr. &
Tetuan for water & provns.
Sent the Nimble to
England at night, fine
weather

Thursday Octr. 3rd: 1805
fine weather sent
Euryalus to Cruize under
Cape St. Marys

off Cadiz. Euryalus captured
a Spanish Privateer

Wednesday Octr. 9th. fresh
Breezes Easterly receiv'd an
account from Capt. Black-
wood that the french Ships
had all bent their Topgt. Sails
sent the Pickle to him with
orders to keep a good look out.
sent Adl. Collingwood the
Nelson Touch — at night
Wind Westerly

Thursday Octr. 10th. 1805
fine Wr. Wind Westerly
receiv'd an account that
the Enemy are ready for

Sea and at the very
Harbours Mouth, British
made for [illegible]
British joined from [illegible].
in the Evening the Renommee
frigate & Confounder Brig
sent the Aetna & Confounder
to Gibraltar. at night very
fresh Breezes NW & Rain

Friday Octr: 11th: fresh
Breezes NW

Saturday Octr. 12th: fresh
Breezes Mostly [illegible]
to the Westward ~~[illegible]~~
~~[illegible]~~

wrote Sr. J.

Sunday Oct. 13th 1805

fine weather Agamem-

-non joined from

England having fallen

in with the French

Squadron off Cape Finist.

consisting of 1 three decker

and 5 two decked ships

and had a narrow

escape from Capture

L'Amazon also joined

who had likewise been

chased Prince of Wales

sailed for England

Monday Oct. 14th:
fine Weather Westerly
Wind sent amphion
to Gibralter & Algiers
enemy at the Harbours
mouth placed Defence &
agamemnon from Seven
to Ten Leagues West of Cadiz
and Mars Colossus five
Leagues East from the
fleet whose Station will be
from 15 Lgs: to twenty West
of Cadiz and by this Chain
I hope to have a constant
communication with the

frigates off Cadiz

Tuesday Oct. 15th fine & Mod.
Westerly sent Renommee
& Aimable to Gibraltar
& Malta. and the transp.s
& Lis.t adv.e Louis is order'd
to see the Convoy above
Carthagena & the frigates
to escort them to Malta.
all night Mod.t Breez.
Westerly

Wednesday Oct. 16th.
Mod.t Breezes Westerly
all the forenoon employ'd
forming the fleet into the

order of Sailing at noon
fresh Breezes WNW & Squally
in the evening fresh gales
Enemy as before. by Sigls.
from Weazle

Thursday Ocr. 17th. 1805
Modt. Breezes NWerly
Sent Donegal to Gibraltar
to get a ground Tier of Casks
received accounts by the
Diligent Store Ship that
Sir Richard Strachan was
supposed in Sight of the
French Rochfort Squadron
which I hope is true

at midnight the wind came
to the Eastward

---

friday Oct. 18th fine weather
wind Easterly the combined
fleets cannot come from W.
Shut to Sea

Saturday Oct. 19th fine Wr.
Wind Easterly at ½ pt 9
the Mars being one of the
look out Ships made the
Signal that the Enemy were
coming out of Port made the
Signal for a General Chase
SE. Wind at South Cadiz
bearing ESE by Compass
distance 16 Leagues

24

at three the Colossus made
the Signal that the Enemys
fleet was at Sea in the
Evening made Sig to Observe
my motions during the
night, for the Britannia
Prince & Dreadnought they
being heavy Sailers to take
Stations as Convenient
and for Mars, Orion Belleisle
Leviathan, Bellerophon &
Polyphemus to go ahead
during the night and to
carry a light standing
for the Streights mouth

at 5 Telegraphed Capt. B:
that I relyed upon his
keeping sight of the Enemy
at 5 O'Clock Naiad made
the signal for 31 Sail of
the Enemy N.N.E. the
frigates and Look out
Ships kept sight of the
Enemy most admirably
all night and told me
by Signals which tack
they were upon. at
8 We wore & stood to the
SW and at 4 ~~o'clock~~ wore

and stood to the NE.

Monday Octr 21st 1805
at day Light saw the
Enemys Combined fleet
from East to ESE bore
away made the Signal
for order of Sailing and
to Prepare for Battle the
Enemy with their heads
to the Southward, at 7
the Enemy wearing in
succession. May the Great
God whom I worship
Grant

to my Country and for
the benefit of Europe
in General a great and
Glorious Victory, and may
no misconduct in any
one tarnish it, and
may humanity after
Victory be the predomi-
-nant feature in the
British fleet, For
myself individually
I commit my Life
to Him who made

me, and may his blessing light upon my endeavours for serving my Country faithfully. To Him I resign myself and the Just cause which is entrusted to me to

Defend—

amen. amen. amen

October the Twenty first one thousand Eight hundred and five then in sight of the Combined fleets of France and Spain distant about Ten Miles.

Whereas the Eminent Services of Emma Hamilton Widow of the Right Honorable Sir William Hamilton have been of the very greatest Service to our King & Country to my

knowledge without our
receiving any reward
from either our King
or Country, just that he
obtaind the King of Spain
letter in 1796 to his
Brother the King of
Naples acquainting him
of his intention to Declare
War against England
from which letter the
ministry sent out orders
to then Sir John Jervis
to strike a stroke of oppr:

tunity offered against
either the arsenals of
Spain or her fleets. That
neither of these was done
is not the fault of Lady
Hamilton the opportu-
-nity might have been
offered. Secondly the British
fleet under my Com-
-mand could never have
returned the second time
to Egypt had not Lady
Hamiltons influence
with the Queen of Naples

caused Letters to be wrote
to the Governor of Syracuse
that he was to encourage
the fleet being supplied
with every thing should
they put into any Port
in Sicily. We put into
Syracuse and received
every supply went to
Egypt & destroyed the
French fleet. Could I have
rewarded these services I
would not now call upon
my Country but as that

has not been in my
power I leave Emma
Lady Hamilton therefore
a Legacy to my King and
Country that they will
give her an ample
provision to maintain
her Rank in Life. I
also leave to the benefi:
:cence of my Country
my adopted daughter
Horatia Nelson Thomp:
:son and I desire she
will

use in future the name
of Nelson only. these
are the only favors I
ask of my King and
Country at this moment
when I am going to
fight their Battle
May God Bless my
King & Country and
all those who I hold
dear My Relations
it is needless to mention

they will of course be
amply provided for
Nelson & Bronte

Witness

Henry Blackwood

T. M. Hardy

Proved at London the 11th day of July
1806 before the Right Honorable Sir William
Scott Knt Dr of Laws & Surrogate by the Oaths
of The Reverend & Right Honorable William
Nelson Dr in Divinity Viscount Merton & Earl
Nelson of Trafalgar & William Haslewood
Esqr the Exors named in the will to whom
Admon was granted having been first
Sworn duly to admr. The will with seven
Codicils was Proved the 23. of December
last by the said Executors./

Will & Cods.
regd Decr 1805

NELSON'S PRAYER

Stood to the NE

Monday Octr 21st a 1805
at day light saw the
Enemys Combined fleet
from East to ESE bore
away made the Signal
for order of Sailing and
to prepare for Battle the
Enemy with their heads
to the Southward at 7
the Enemy wearing in
succession May the Great
God whom I worship
Grant

to my Country and for
the benefit of Europe
in General a great and
Glorious Victory, and may
no misconduct in any
one tarnish it and
may humanity after
Victory be the predomi
nant feature in the
British fleet, For
myself individually
I commit my Life
to Him who made

me and may his blessing
light upon my endea
vours for serving my
Country faithfully, to
Him I resign myself
and the Just cause which
is entrusted to me to
Defend
Amen Amen Amen

and stood to the NE.

Monday Octr 21st 1805
at day Light saw the
Enemys Combined fleet
from East to ESE bore
away made the Signal
for order of Sailing and
to Prepare for Battle the
Enemy with their heads
to the Southward, at 7
the Enemy wearing in
succession, May the Great
God whom I worship
Grant

to my Country and for
the benefit of Europe
in General a great and
Glorious Victory, and may
no misconduct in any
one tarnish it, and
may humanity after
Victory be the predomi-
-nant feature in the
British fleet, For
myself individually
I commit my Life
to Him who made

me, and may his blessing
light upon my endea-
-vours for serving my
Country faithfully, to
Him I resign myself
and the Just cause which
is entrusted to me to
Defend_
amen. amen. amen

The Public Record Office copy

125

Victory Octr: 19th: 1805
Noon Cadiz ESE 16 Leagues

My Dearest beloved Emma the dear
friend of my bosom the Signal has
been made that the Enemys Combined
fleet are coming out of Port, We
have very little Wind so that I have
no hopes of seeing them before tomorrow
May the God of Battles crown my
Endeavours with success at all events
I will take care that my name shall ever
be most dear to you and Horatia both
of whom I love as much as my own
life, and as my last writing before the
battle will be to you so I hope in God that
I shall live to finish my letter after the

Battle, may Heaven bless you prays
your Nelson & Bronte. Octr. 20th: in the
morning we were close to the mouth of the
Streights but the Wind had not come far
enough to the Westward to allow the Combined
fleets to Weather the Shoals off Trafalgar but
they were counted as far as forty Sail of Ships
of War which I suppose to be 34 of the Line
and Six frigates, a Group of them was
seen off the Lighthouse of Cadiz this Morng
but it blows so very fresh & thick weather
that I rather believe they will go into
the Harbour before Night, May God
almighty give us success over these fellows

126

and enable us to get a Peace

This letter was found open on
His desk & brought to
Lady Hamilton by
Capn Hardy

oh miserable wretched
Emma
oh glorious & happy Nelson

NOTES

Dates refer to entries in the Diary:

13/14 *September* 1805
Merton, near Wimbledon, was not far from the London-Portsmouth road, now the A.3. When Nelson eventually reached Portsdown Hill, overlooking Portsmouth Harbour, he was close to a spot where in 1807 (long before the Napoleonic War was over) his companions in arms erected a 150 foot column to his memory, subscribed for out of their Trafalgar prize-money. Merton has long vanished; not so the column.

GEORGE ROSE (1744-1818). Originally in the Navy. Secretary to the Treasury 1782-3 and 1784-1801. Master of Pleas in the Court of Exchequor. Vice-President, Board of Trade, 1804-6. Treasurer of the Navy 1807-12.

GEORGE CANNING (1770-1827). Under Secretary for Foreign Affairs 1796-9. Treasurer of the Navy 1804-6. Foreign Secretary 1822. Prime Minister 1827.

16 *September*
At this and various other dates Nelson noted that he wrote to Lady Hamilton, though when the letters went off depended on the exigencies of the Service. A missive bearing this date is printed in the *Memoirs of the Life of Vice-Admiral Lord Viscount Nelson* by Thomas Joseph Pettigrew, 2 Vols (1849) hereafter referred to as Pettigrew. The reference in this case is II.498. " We have a fair wind," wrote Nelson, " and God will, I hope, soon grant us a happy meeting." Also II.499, written from off Portland expressing the hope that Nelson would not have to anchor off Weymouth, where George III was staying: " but should I be forced, I shall act as a man, and your Nelson, neither courting nor ashamed to hold up my head before the greatest monarch in the world. I have, thank God, nothing to be ashamed of."

18 *September*
Pettigrew II.499 prints letters dated 17 and 18 September in the first of which Nelson writes: " I intreat, my dear Emma, that you will cheer up, and we will look forward to many many happy years, and can be surrounded by our children. God Almighty can, when he pleases, remove the impediment "—the reference is of course to Lady Nelson. " My heart and soul is with you and Horatia." The second letter was composed ' Off the Lizard '. Nelson writes: " Perseverance has got us thus far, and the same will, I dare say, get us on."

20 *September*
A letter bearing this date was printed in *The Hamilton and Nelson Papers*, a collection of documents assembled by Alfred Morrison and privately printed, 2 Vols (1893-4) hereafter referred to as Morrison. The *Victory* was then SW of the Isles of Scilly and Nelson had begun to fear that a battle might already have been fought off the Spanish coast. If so, he added, " I shall be sadly vexed but I cannot help myself."

CHARLES STIRLING (1760-1833). Rear Admiral, 1804. Stirling had taken part under Sir Robert Calder in an action with the Franco-Spanish Fleet under Villeneuve fought in July 1805, without decisive result. Stirling was then on his way home. He became a Vice-Admiral in 1810 but four years later was placed on half pay for corruption.

SIR RICHARD BICKERTON (1759-1832). In 1805 Bickerton was a Rear Admiral of five years seniority who had seen much service under Nelson in the Mediterranean and elsewhere, though he missed Trafalgar. He became a full Admiral in 1810 and later Commander-in-Chief, Portsmouth.

25 *September*
In Pettigrew II.500 there is a letter from Nelson written off Lisbon and bearing this date in which he says: " I am anxious to join the Fleet, for it would add to my grief if any other man was to give them the Nelson touch, which we say is warranted never to fail."

26 *September*

CUTHBERT COLLINGWOOD (1748-1810). Rear Admiral, 1799. Vice-Admiral, 1804. Nelson's second-in-command was the oldest and best friend of his Service life. They had served together in the West Indies and the Mediterranean and had that mutual trust resulting from trial by battle, for they had fought close to one another at St Vincent in 1797. It fell to Collingwood to write the Trafalgar despatch, and to continue Nelson's work in the Mediterranean and Atlantic. Collingwood never again saw his Northumbrian home, but died, a martyr to duty, at sea off Minorca, five years before the war was over.

1 *October*

SIR THOMAS LOUIS (1759-1807). Rear Admiral, 1804. Louis, a descendant of the Kings of France, was a special favourite of Nelson, under whom he fought at the Nile. He missed Trafalgar owing to having to provision his ship at Gibraltar, but served with distinction under Admiral Duckworth at San Domingo in 1806.

13 *October*

By this date letters to Emma seem to have been accumulating. Morrison II.267 prints one dated 1 October in which Nelson wrote: " I am sensible that the Ministry are sending me all the force they can, and I hope to use it." Next day he added: " I have had, as you will believe, a very distressing scene with poor Sir Robert Calder. He has wrote home to beg an enquiry, feeling confident that he can fully justify himself. I sincerely hope he may, but—I have given him the advice as to my dearest friend. He is now in adversity, and if he ever has been my enemy, he now feels the pang of it, and finds me one of his best friends."

SIR ROBERT CALDER (1745-1818). Rear Admiral, 1799. Calder had fought creditably against Villeneuve off Finisterre on 22 July 1805 but the Admiralty and the public were distressed that the engagement had not been renewed next day. Calder, hurt and enraged, asked for an Enquiry into his conduct. This was duly granted but it resulted in a reprimand which many thought unjust. Calder was suspected of jealousy of Nelson, and forfeited all claim to sympathy when, after being sent home in his own flag-ship, the three-decked *Prince of Wales*, he had the effrontery to claim to share in the Trafalgar prize-money. He afterwards became Commander-in-Chief at Plymouth.

17 *October*
SIR RICHARD STRACHAN (1760-1828). Known as " the delighted Sir Dickie " from the dispatch he wrote home after a successful action on 4 November 1805 in which he captured French ships of the line, four in number, which had escaped Nelson's onslaught at Trafalgar.

20 *October*
The reference in Nicolas, *Dispatches and Letters of Vice Admiral Lord Viscount Nelson:* 7 Vols. (1844-6) is VII.136-7. It runs:
" Fresh breezes SSW and rainy. Communicated with Phoebe, Defence and Colossus, who saw near forty Sail of Ships of War outside of Cadiz yesterday evening: but the wind being Southerly, they could not get to the Mouth of the Straits. We were between Trafalgar and Cape Spartel. The Frigates made the signal that they saw 9 Sail outside the Harbour; gave the Frigates instructions for their guidance, and placed Defence, Colossus and Mars between me and the Frigates. At noon fresh gales and heavy rain, Cadiz N.E. 9 leagues. In the afternoon Captain Blackwood telegraphed that the Enemy seemed determined to go to the Westward: and that they shall *not* do if in the power of Nelson and Bronte to prevent them."

Affidavit
ALEXANDER JOHN SCOTT (1768-1840). Educated at Charterhouse and St John's College, Cambridge. Served at sea under Admiral Sir Hyde Parker at Copenhagen in 1801. Scott was multilingual, and was invaluable to Nelson during his tenure of the Mediterranean command. Chaplain of the *Victory* and a central figure at Nelson's obsequies. Little was done for Scott until 1816, when he was made Chaplain to the Prince Regent.

Nelson was engaged on a letter to Emma Hamilton on 19 and 20 October, 1805, but this was never despatched, and it was found open on his desk after the battle. It is printed in full herein from British Museum: Egerton MS 1614ff.125-6, including Emma's post-script. The reference in Nicolas is VII.132.

Post-script

By a curious chance the present editor found in a local second-hand book-shop a copy of Gilbert Hudson's printed version of the Diary, while this work was in proof. The copy contained two corrections in Hudson's handwriting. The first refers to the entry for October 3rd 1805, which Hudson had noted as being a Monday: actually it was a Thursday. The second was more important, for on October 15 Hudson printed that the *Warspite* had been sent to Gibraltar, along with two other ships. It happened that the *Warspite* of 1758 was renamed *Arundel* in 1800 and she was not in fact in the area at the time. The word should be ' transports ', as can be seen from Nelson's holograph.